Howler Monkeys

By Sandra Donovan

Raintree

A Division of Reed Elsevier, Inc.

Chicago, Illinois

www.raintreelibrary.com

ANIMALS OF THE RAIN FOREST

For information, address the publisher:
Raintree, 100 N. LaSalle, Suite 1200, Chicago, IL 60602

Library of Congress Cataloging-in-Publication Data
Donovan, Sandra.
  Howler monkeys / Sandra Donovan.
      p. cm. -- (Animals of the rain forest)
Includes bibliographical references (p.   ).
  ISBN 978-0-7398-6836-2 (0-7398-6836-5) (HC)
  1. Howler monkeys--Juvenile literature. I. Title. II. Series.
  QL737.P925 D65 2003
  599.8'55--dc21
                                        2002015209
Printed and bound in the United States of America

Produced by Compass Books

Photo Acknowledgments
Unicorn/Robert Barber, cover, 1, 8; Visuals Unlimited/James Beveridge, 11; Luiz Claudio Marigo, 6, 12, 16, 18, 26; Wildlife Conservation Society/Elyssa Kellerman, 14; World Wildlife Fund/Tony Rath, 21, 22; Visuals Unlimited/Rob Simpson, 25; Root Resources/Kenneth W. Fink, 28-29.

Content Consultants
Dennis R. Rasmussen, Ph.D.
President, Primate Foundation of Panama and Director, Primate Refuge and Sanctuary of Panama

Ing. I. Broekema, Secretary Primate Foundation of Panama and Development Manager of the Primate Refuge and Sanctuary of Panama

Mark Rosenthal
Abra Prentice Wilkin Curator of Large Mammals
Lincoln Park Zoo, Chicago, Illinois

This book supports the National Science Standards.

Some words are shown in bold, **like this**. You can find out what they mean by looking in the Glossary.

Contents

Range Map of Howler Monkeys. 4

A Quick Look at Howler Monkeys. 5

Howler Monkeys in the Rain Forest. 7

What Howler Monkeys Eat. 15

A Howler Monkeys Life Cycle. 19

The Future of Howler Monkeys. 25

Photo Diagram. 28

Glossary. 30

Internet Sites, Address, Books to Read. 31

Index. 32

Range Map of Howler Monkeys

MEXICO

BELIZE
HONDURAS
GUATEMALA
EL SALVADOR
NICARAGUA

North
Atlantic
Ocean

Caribbean
Sea

COSTA RICA

PANAMA

ECUADOR

COLOMBIA

VENEZUELA

GUYANA
SURINAME

FRENCH
GUIANA
(FRANCE)

PERU

AMAZON
RIVER

BRAZIL

Range of the
Howler
Monkeys

Surrounding
Land

Water

Borders

Rivers

BOLIVIA

South
Pacific
Ocean

PARAGUAY

CHILE

South
Atlantic
Ocean

ARGENTINA

URUGUAY

N
W · E
S

A Quick Look at Howler Monkeys

What do howler monkeys look like?

Howler monkeys have a hairless face with a thick, short nose. They also have a saggy chin with a large lower jaw. Their tail is longer than their body. Each kind of howler monkey has different colored fur.

Where do howler monkeys live?

Howler monkeys live only in the rain forests of North America, Central America, and South America. They live in many different countries, including Mexico, Belize, Brazil, Argentina, Panama, Costa Rica, Paraguay, Guatemala, and Bolivia.

What do howler monkeys eat?

Howler monkeys eat mainly leaves. They also eat fruit that they find. Sometimes they eat bugs.

All howler monkeys belong to a larger scientific group called Alouatta.

Howler Monkeys in the Rain Forest

If you visited a rain forest, you would most likely hear howler monkeys long before you see them. People hear the screaming calls of these monkeys up to 3 miles (4.8 kilometers) away. Their calls are among the loudest sounds that any animal can make.

Scientists do not agree about the number of species of howler monkeys. A species is a kind of animal that mates mainly with other members of its species. Most agree that there are seven species of howler monkeys. These species are red-handed, Coiba Island, brown, mantled, black, Guatemalan, and red howler. Each species of monkey is named after their color or the place they live.

▲ Howler monkeys spend most of their lives
eating and sleeping in high trees.

Where do howler monkeys live?

Howler monkeys are New World monkeys.
New World monkeys live in North America,
South America, and Central America. Other kinds
of monkeys live in Europe, Asia, and Africa.
These are called Old World monkeys.

Howler monkeys live only in the rain forests
of North America, Central America, and South

America. In the rain forest, trees grow close together and a lot of rain falls. Howler monkeys live in the rain forests of many different countries, including Mexico, Belize, Brazil, Argentina, Panama, Costa Rica, Paraguay, Guatemala, and Bolivia.

The rain forest **canopy** is the **habitat** of howler monkeys. A habitat is the place where a plant or animal usually lives. The canopy is the area of thick leaves and branches high above the ground. Trees there can grow more than 100 feet (30 meters) tall.

Howler monkeys are important to the rain forest since they help spread and plant the seeds of the trees that they eat. The monkeys eat many different kinds of plants in the forest. Some of the plant seeds leave their bodies as waste. New plants can grow from the seeds in the waste. This helps the plants spread to new places.

Howler monkeys usually stay in one area of the canopy for their whole lives. This area is called their home range. A howler monkey's range is usually two to four square miles (five to ten square kilometers). In this space, it lives and looks for food.

What do howler monkeys look like?

The size of a howler monkey depends on what species it is. Most howler monkeys are less than 2 feet (0.6 meters) in length. They weigh from 10 to 20 pounds (4.6 to 9 kilograms). The black howler monkey is the biggest and heaviest monkey in the Americas. The male black howler may weigh 20 pounds (9 kilograms).

Different species of howler monkeys have different colored fur. For example, red howler monkeys have reddish fur. Brown howler monkeys have brown fur. But only adult male black howler monkeys have all-black fur.

Females and males of the same kind do not always look alike. As adults, females are smaller than males and often have different colored fur.

Howler monkeys do not have fur on their faces. They have thick, short noses. They also have saggy chins with large lower jaws. Behind this saggy chin is a wide, egg-shaped bone. Howler monkeys use this bone to make their loud howling sounds.

Howler monkeys have strong **prehensile** tails. Prehensile means able to grab and hold. They can use their tails to grab onto branches while

▲ **This black howler monkey is using its thumbs to help it hold onto the branch.**

moving and feeding high in the **canopy**. A howler will sometimes hang from a branch only by its tail. Howlers' tails are longer than their bodies!

Howler monkeys also use their hands and feet to move around the trees. They have long arms. Their hands have four fingers and a thumb. The thumb is opposite from the four fingers on the hand. This means they can grab objects. Only humans, monkeys, and apes have thumbs.

These two howler monkeys are members of the same group.

How do howler monkeys act?

Howler monkeys are social animals. This means that males, females, and their young live together in a group.

Each group may have between 5 and 50 howler monkeys. Some species of howler monkeys live in larger groups than others. The size of the group also depends on how many are in one area. There are usually at least 2 males and 3 or 4 females in a group. The rest of the members of the group are young howler monkeys. Sometimes a group may be made up of young males. This group may fight with other groups to get females.

One member of the group is usually the leader. At times this may be an older female. Usually a younger adult male is the **dominant** member of the group. Dominant means he is most powerful. He leads the group, and the other members follow him.

Howler monkeys have different ways to **communicate**. They use noises to send messages to each other and to other groups. They howl or growl to warn other groups to stay away from their homes. Females screech if they cannot find their young. If a howler is upset, it may grunt. The leader makes clicking noises to tell the group where to go.

Howler monkeys spend a small part of their time **grooming**. Grooming means cleaning oneself or someone else. Dominant members of the group groom those that are not as powerful. They may lick them or pick bugs from their fur.

This howler monkey is eating fruit that it has found.

What Howler Monkeys Eat

Almost all howler monkeys are **herbivores**. This means they only eat plants. Very few howler monkeys eat animals. When they do, they usually only eat small bugs.

Howler monkeys mostly eat leaves. Up to 75 percent of their diet is made up of leaves. They eat more leaves than any other New World monkey. They also eat other plant parts, like seeds, flowers, and fruit. Small berries and figs are favorite howler monkey meals.

Howler monkeys also need water to survive. Sometimes they climb down from the **canopy** to drink from rivers or ponds. They also get water when it rains. Rain water collects in holes in trees and in curled leaves. Howlers drink from these "cups" and they also rub their hands on wet leaves and lick their fingers.

This howler monkey is about to eat a leaf from the tree.

Finding food and eating

Howler monkeys prefer to eat the leaves they find in the rain forest **canopy**. They can reach for these leaves with one or two hands while they hang onto a branch with their feet or their tail.

Usually, howler monkeys do not have to look far to find food. The kinds of plants they eat grow in many places in the rain forest. During the dry season, food may be hard to find. They might have to travel farther to find leaves.

Sometimes there is more fruit in the rain forests than usual. This happens because of **mass fruiting**. Mass fruiting is when most of the fruit trees grow fruit at the same time. This happens about every three to seven years. At this time, food is easier for howler monkeys to find.

Howler monkeys have bodies that are well suited for eating plants. Special bacteria in their stomachs break down leaves into nutrients they need for energy. This allows them to eat leaves that other animals cannot.

All animals eat food to get energy. Howler monkeys eat many leaves, but they do not get much energy. This is because leaves do not provide very much nutrition. Nutrition is energy that animals get from food. Because howler monkeys do not get a lot of energy from food, they do not move around very much.

After they are two years old, young howler monkeys take care of themselves.

A Howler Monkey's Life Cycle

When females are about three years old, they begin to mate and have babies. They usually mate with **dominant** males from their group. A female howler monkey may have one baby every two years. Sometimes one female will have about ten babies in ten years.

Howler monkeys may mate at any time during the year. Females show special signs when they are ready to mate. Their skin may swell and look pink. They sometimes flick their tongues at males.

After mating, the male and female stay with the rest of the group. About five months later, the female gives birth. She usually has only one baby at a time.

A hyoid (HYE-oyd) bone sits at the base of the howler monkey's tongue. A howler's jaw is also a wide bone. When it moves these two bones at the same time, it makes a loud hoot sound. When some of this sound gets trapped in his its throat, it becomes the howl these monkeys are known for.

Young howler monkeys

When a baby howler monkey is born it lives with its mother's group. After birth, a baby clings to its mother's stomach fur. This keeps it warm. As it gets older, the baby moves to its mother's back. It wraps its tail around its mother's tail so it stays on as the mother moves through the treetops. It rides around like this for almost a year.

For the first few months, the mothers **nurse** their babies every two to three hours. Nursing is when a baby drinks milk that the mother makes in her body. Soon the baby learns how to find food on its own. It learns by watching the types of food selected by its mother and other group members.

▲ **This young howler monkey is old enough to move around on its own.**

When they are 2 years old, young howler monkeys are fully grown. They begin to take care of themselves.

Both females and males may leave their mother's group to find a new group. Sometimes they live alone for a while. Once they join another group and mate, they do not return to their parents' group. Howler monkeys may live for 20 years.

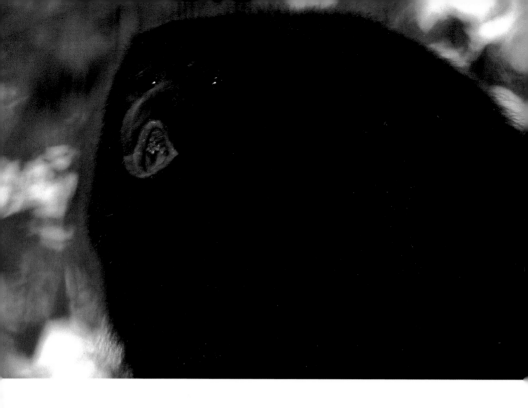

Any loud noise, such as thunder, may make a group start howling.

A howler monkey's day

Howler monkeys are **diurnal**. This means they are active during the day and sleep at night. At night a group of howler monkeys sleeps close together, high in the trees.

They wake up when the sun rises. Usually howler monkeys make their loudest calls the first thing in the morning. Their roar lets other groups know their location. It is a warning to stay away. Sometimes two groups may argue back and forth with one another. Then, they may howl for hours.

After the morning howl, a group of howler monkeys begins to gather food. They can usually find leaves and plants in the same trees they slept in. After eating, howler monkeys often rest. They spend about three-quarters of their time resting.

Throughout the day, howler monkeys must protect themselves from **predators**. A predator is an animal that hunts other animals and eats them. Large birds like harpy eagles often hunt and eat howler monkeys.

To protect themselves, howler monkeys may scream. Sometimes the loud noise scares away predators. They also try to avoid being spotted by predators. They do this by blending into the trees. For example, a brown howler monkey may look like a clump of dead, brown leaves. Predators have a hard time finding them.

At night, the howler monkeys travel back to a sleeping site. They may howl and call to each other as they travel, or to let other groups know where they are sleeping. When morning comes, they begin the cycle all over again.

Without rain forests, howler monkeys will not be able to find the food they need.

The Future of Howler Monkeys

For thousands of years, howler monkeys have lived in rain forests. In rain forests, howler monkeys can find plenty to eat. They can also blend in so predators cannot find them.

Today, rain forests are being destroyed. People are tearing down the trees to clear the land for farming. Other people are putting roads through the rain forests.

These activities destroy the natural **habitat** of many animals like howler monkeys. Without rain forests, the animals have nowhere to live. They will not be able to find enough food to eat. If this happens, the animals will die.

▲ Howler monkeys can jump from tree to tree to travel around the forest canopy.

What will happen to howler monkeys?

Hunting puts howler monkeys at risk, too. Many hunters try to catch howler monkeys for their meat. Baby howler monkeys are often caught alive to be sold as pets. Sadly, most of these pets die. People who buy them do not know how to care for them. They cannot give them enough kinds of fresh leaves to eat.

Because of hunting and **habitat** loss, some kinds of howler monkeys are **endangered**. Endangered means at risk of dying out.

Howler monkeys need the rain forests to live. Many people are working to save the rain forests for animals. They are trying to pass laws that stop people from cutting down trees in the rain forest. Some countries in South America and Central America already have laws like this.

People in other countries are working to save the howler monkey. In Belize, people have saved land along the Belize River for howler monkeys. A group of people worked to pass a law that says people cannot cut down trees on this land. Today many howler monkeys live there safely.

In Panama people started the Primate Refuge and Sanctuary of Panama. Scientists there treat howler monkeys that have been pets. They train them and set them free in their natural habitat.

More work is needed to save the rain forest for animals like the howler monkey. Some people try to teach others how to use the land without destroying it. Then the rain forest can remain home to many animals.

saggy chin
see page 10

opposable thumb
see page 11

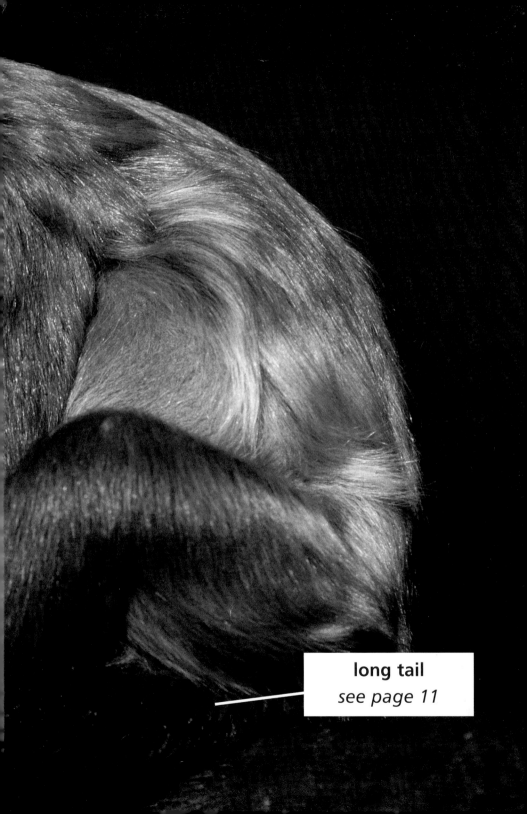

long tail
see page 11

Glossary

canopy—an area of thick leaves high level in the rain forest where trees grow close together

communicate—to make thoughts or ideas known to others

diurnal—animals that sleep at night and are active during the day

dominant—powerful leader

endangered—at risk of dying out

energy—the force in nature that lets plants and animals grow

grooming—the act of cleaning oneself or another's body

habitat—the place where an animal or plant usually lives

herbivores—animals that eat only plants and tree parts

mass fruiting—when most of the fruit trees in the rain forest grow fruit at the same time

nursing—when a mother feeds her young the milk made inside her body

prehensile—able to hold or grasp

Internet Sites

Belize Zoo—Black Howler Monkey
http://www.belizezoo.org/zoo/zoo/mammals/how
/how1.html

Howler Monkeys
http://www.stri.org/F_Speak/en/mammals4.htm

Useful Address

Howler Monkey Exhibit
Central Park Wildlife Center
830 Fifth Avenue
New York, NY 10021

Books to Read

Harman, Amanda. *New World Monkeys.*
Danbury, Conn.: Grolier Educational, 2001.

Reid, Mary. *Howlers and Other New World Monkeys.* Chicago: World Book, 2000.

Index

bacteria 17

Belize 4, 5, 9, 27

Brazil 4, 5, 9

canopy 9, 11, 15, 16, 26, 30

Central America 4, 5, 8, 27

communicate 13, 30

diurnal 22, 30

dominant 13, 19, 30

endangered 27, 30

energy 17

grooming 13, 30

habitat 9, 25, 27, 30

herbivores 15, 30

mass fruiting 17, 30

mating 19

Mexico 4, 5, 9

nursing 20, 30

prehensile 10, 30

South America 4, 5, 8, 9, 27

species 7, 10, 12